ARIES
March 21–April 19

I am no bird
and no net
ensnares me
I am a free
human being
with an
independent will

☆ Charlotte Brontë, *Jane Eyre* ☆

POPPY

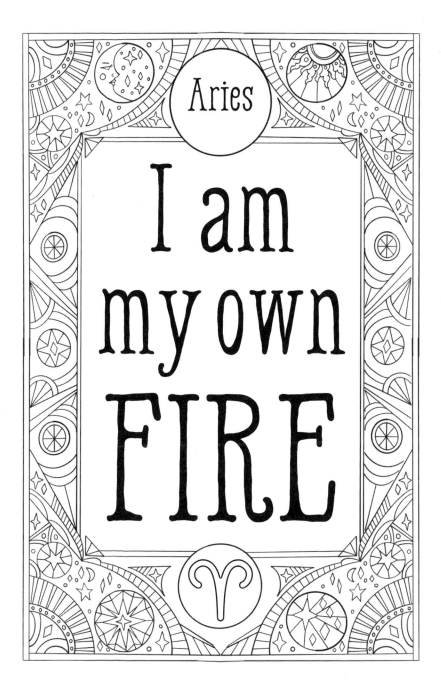

spring

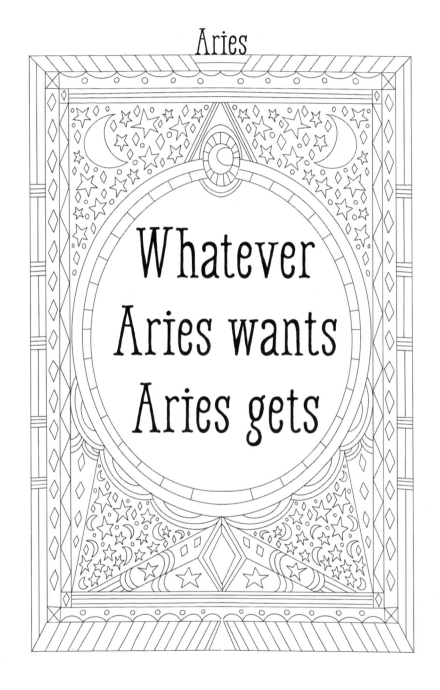

Whatever
Aries wants
Aries gets

ARIES

Ruled by Mars

RULING HOUSE

HOUSE

1

The House of Self

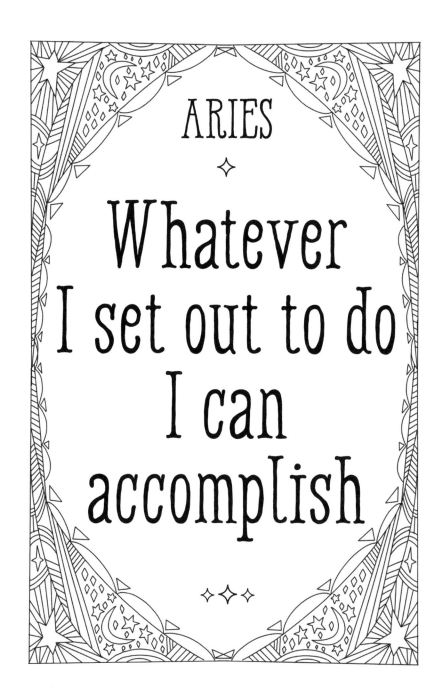

ARIES

✦

Whatever I set out to do I can accomplish

✦✦✦

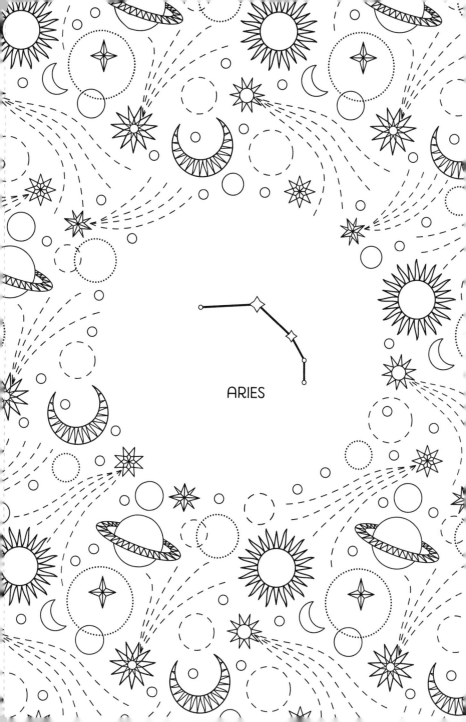

ARIES

Aries

Taurus

Gemini

Cancer

Leo

Virgo

Libra

Scorpio

Sagittarius

Capricorn

Aquarius

Pisces

Fire Signs

Aries

Leo

Sagittarius

LET THE STARS LEAD THE WAY